THE MAN IN THE RED BANDANNA
By Honor Crowther Fagan
Illustrated by John Crowther

A Publication of
The Welles Remy Crowther Charitable Trust

Dedicated to Welles Remy Crowther and all the men, women and children who lost their lives on September 11, 2001, their families and friends.

A Publication of The Welles Remy Crowther Charitable Trust
P.O. Box 780, Nyack, NY 10960
www.crowthertrust.org

This work was supported by the Fetzer Institute

ISBN-13: 978-1481961929 (CreateSpace-Assigned)
ISBN-10: 1481961926

When he was only 7 years old, Welles was given a bandanna by his father. It was a special gift that made Welles feel strong.

Welles' dad always carried a blue bandanna and Welles'
new bandanna was just like it... only red!

From the moment Welles received that bandanna, he carried it with him everywhere.

It had lots of uses. It was a cowboy mask .....

.... a pirate hat ....

.... a flag to signal the end of the race.

As Welles grew up, he stopped using his red bandanna as
a toy and started to use it underneath his helmets.

You see, Welles was an athlete, whose favorite sports were ice hockey and lacrosse. He wore that bandanna underneath his helmet to keep the sweat out of his eyes.

Welles not only wore a helmet when he played sports, he also wore one as a volunteer firefighter.

At the age of 16, Welles again followed his father's example and became a volunteer fireman. He trained with real firefighters and was taught that rescuing people who were trapped inside was their first priority. He also learned how to get safely through the burning building and put out the fires.

It was this training and the red bandanna that helped Welles become a hero.

After college, Welles went to work on the 104th floor of the World Trade Center in New York City. Welles loved working up so high. He often called his father on rainy days to ask, "Is it raining where you are?" When his father replied that it was, Welles would say, "Well, it's sunny up here!"

But on Tuesday morning, September 11, 2001, it was not a rainy day. The sun was bright and there were no clouds in the blue sky.

As Welles sat in his office, he heard an explosion nearby that rattled his desk and his chair. When he looked out the window to see the World Trade Center Tower 1 building, he could see fire spewing out of the floors right across from him.

Welles wanted to help with the tragic situation unfolding in the next tower. Just minutes after the explosion in Tower 1, Welles left his office.

To get down to the lobby from above the 78th floor, you had to first take an elevator to the 78th Floor Sky Lobby. From there, you took a non-stop elevator to the ground floor. Many people would be waiting in the Sky Lobby for their elevator.

Welles knew it would take too long to wait for an elevator from the 104th floor to the Sky Lobby and then one to the ground, so he headed down the stairs.

In a few minutes, Welles had made it all the way down near the 78th Floor. That's when another explosion occurred. Only this one was much louder and stronger than the last.

Welles ran right for the door of the Sky Lobby,
but could tell by the smoke coming into the
stairwell that there were fires burning inside.

Welles took out his red bandanna and tied it
around his nose and mouth, so that he did not
breathe in the smoke.

When Welles entered the Sky Lobby, it was hard to see
through all the smoke. There were
badly injured people who needed his help to get to safety.

He found a fire extinguisher to put out the flames
that continued to endanger the survivors.

Welles immediately took charge and called out to anyone who might be able to hear him, "I found the stairs. If you can get up and walk, get up now. If you are able to help someone else, help them... follow me, I know the way."

Many people were dazed but one woman was in such a state of shock that she could not walk. Welles wanted to help as many survivors as possible. He picked up the shocked woman and, leading a group of three others, carried her down the stairs.

Welles saw the air start to clear as they made it down the stairwell, so he pulled his bandanna from his face. When they made it to the 61st floor, the lights were on and Welles thought it was safe to send the people on their own.

Welles told the group to continue down the stairs and out of the building. He turned around and headed back up the stairs.

Welles collected another group of survivors and ushered them to the stairs. Again, he led them down to the clean air on the 61st floor and told them to continue on to safety. Once again, Welles went back up the stairs.

During his third trip to the Sky Lobby, Welles found that there were people who were alive, but were trapped underneath heavy pieces of metal. He knew that in order to save them, he would need a firefighters' tool called a "jaws of life."

Welles followed the stairs down to the lobby for his third and final trip. He found the Command Center where firefighters and police officers were planning the rescue effort. Welles let them know that they would need the "jaws of life" up in the Sky Lobby ....

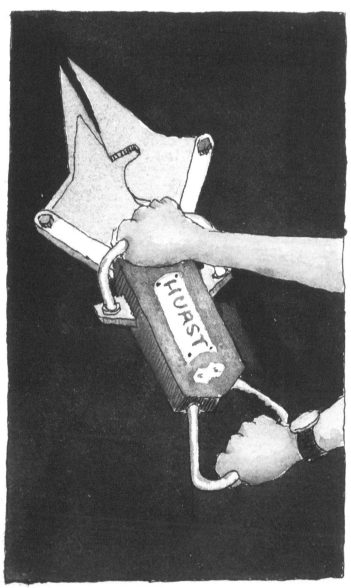

.... but Welles would not make it back up there. The damage to both buildings was too severe and they soon collapsed.

No one knew what had happened to Welles until his mother read a newspaper article, months later. In the article, survivors recalled being saved by a man in a red bandanna. She said to herself, "There you are Welles, I have finally found you!"

away. Her arm fractured in the crash, Mrs. Spira could still walk.

A mysterious **man appeared at one point, his mouth and nose covered with a red handkerchief.** He was looking for a fire extinguisher. As Judy Wein recalls, he pointed to the stairs and made an announcement that saved lives: Anyone who can walk, get up and walk now. Anyone who can perhaps help others, find someone who needs help and then head down.

In groups of two and three, the survivors struggled to the stairs. A few flights down, they propped up debris blocking their way, leaving a small passageway to slip through.

re how long ious, on the the express of stirring is

chard brielle

A few minutes behind this group was Ling Young, who also survived the impact in the sky lobby. **She, too, said she had been steered by the man in the red bandanna,** hearing him call out: "This way to the stairs." He trailed her down the stairs. Ms. Young said she soon noticed that he was carrying a woman on his back. Once they reached clearer air, he put her down and went back up.

Welles was recognized through pictures by two women whom he led to safety. They will never forget the bravery and strength that Welles showed on that day. They will never forget the man who saved their lives. They will never forget ....

.... the man in the red bandanna.

Welles Remy Crowther's three trips from the 78th Floor Sky Lobby to the 61st floor of the World Trade Center's South Tower saved many lives. Because of his bravery and courage on 9/11/01, Welles was posthumously named as an Honorary Firefighter by the Fire Department of New York, the first time in the history of the Department that an individual has been honored in this way. He has been recognized all over the world for his heroic acts through numerous media outlets including ESPN's *Outside the Lines.*

The Welles Remy Crowther Charitable Trust was established in Welles' memory to raise funds for various programs that assist young people to become exemplary adults through education, health, recreation and character development.

A portion of the proceeds from the sale of this book will be donated to the Trust.

The Crowther Family, Trustees and Advisors of the Welles Remy Crowther Charitable Trust are deeply grateful to the Fetzer Institute, Kalamazoo, Michigan for its vision and generous support of this book and the Red Bandanna Project, a curriculum program for character development.

The Welles Remy Crowther Charitable Trust is recognized as a not-for-profit organization under section 501 (c) (3) of the Internal Revenue Service Code.

CPSIA information can be obtained
at www.ICGtesting.com
Printed in the USA
LVHW071637230321
682232LV00004B/15